A Family in Egypt

LIBRARY OF CONGRESS CATALOGING IN PUBLICATION DATA

Bennett, Olivia.
    A family in Egypt.

    Previously published as: Village in Egypt.
    Summary: Describes the life of a ten-year-old
Egyptian boy who lives in a large village near Cairo
with his farmer grandfather, his camel driver father,
and the rest of his extended family.
    1. Egypt—Rural conditions—Juvenile literature.
2. Egypt—Social life and customs—Juvenile literature.
[1. Egypt—Social life and customs] I. Taylor, Liba,
ill. II. Title.
HN786.A8B46   1985   307.7'2'09621   84-19468
ISBN 0-8225-1652-7 (lib. bdg.)

Manufactured in the United States of America

1 2 3 4 5 6 7 8 9 10 94 93 92 91 90 89 88 87 86 85

916.2
Ben
11/85
Prev. Mar

A Family in Egypt

Olivia Bennett
Photographs by Liba Taylor

Lerner Publications Company · Minneapolis

Ezzat is 10 years old. He lives in Om Khenan, a village in Egypt. Every morning before he goes to school, Ezzat feeds his pet goat.

Ezzat's village is about 10½ miles (17 kilometers) from Cairo, Egypt's capital. Both Cairo and Om Khenan are built on the banks of the Nile River. All the water for cooking, washing, drinking, and watering the crops comes from the river. Egypt gets little rain, and almost all Egyptians live near the Nile to be close to water.

Most of Egypt, in fact, is a huge desert. The land cannot be farmed without water, so very few people live there. Some people live in desert oases (oh-AY-sees), small patches of desert where water has come to the surface.

The photograph on the right shows a green strip of land along the banks of the Nile. This is where the crops are grown.

LIBYA

Dakhla Oasis

E   G

N

fertile land

desert

100 km
0   100 miles

Main Roads

MEDITERRANEAN SEA

Alexandria

Port Said

Ismalia

Suez Canal

Cairo

Om Khenan

Suez

SINAI

River Nile

Farafra Oasis

Y P T

El Kharga Oasis

Luxor

RED SEA

SAUDI ARABIA

SUDAN

Mecca

EUROPE

ATLANTIC OCEAN

MEDITERRANEAN SEA

EGYPT

AFRICA

River Nile

Ezzat lives with his mother and father, his younger sister Elham, his grandparents, and his three uncles. One of Ezzat's uncles is married. His wife and children also live in Ezzat's house. Egyptian women often live with their husband's family when they marry.

Ezzat's father is making tea for breakfast. He boils the water and the tea leaves. Then he puts lots of sugar in the pot and pours on the tea. The tea is very strong and sweet. Ezzat's grandmother has made a pastry for breakfast. She holds one of Ezzat's cousins while Ezzat's father and Uncle Khaled eat.

Uncle Abd el Aziz buys his breakfast on the way to work. He stops at Layla's stall in the village square. She is selling freshly baked bread wrapped around fried eggplants, beans, tomatoes, and peppers. People in Egypt often buy their breakfast at stalls like Layla's even in the big cities.

The streets around the square are full of people on their way to work or school. Many of them ride donkeys or bicycles. Others drive horse-drawn carts piled high with sacks of grain. The streets in Om Khenan are very narrow. Families build their houses close together so they don't use up too much precious farmland.

Like many other houses in the village, Ezzat's house is built around a courtyard. It's a good place for cooking, eating, washing, or sitting to talk. A door from the courtyard opens onto the street. At night, the animals are kept in stables inside the courtyard. To steal Ezzat's goat, a thief would have to come right inside the house!

Om Khenan is a large village. About 10,000 people live there. When the village was smaller, all of the villagers were farmers. Today, many of them have jobs in factories, shops, and offices. They work in Cairo or nearby towns. As Egypt's villages and cities grow larger, there is less land to farm. Some farmers have to find other jobs, and some people even have to leave Egypt to find work.

9

Ezzat's grandfather is a farmer and owns about 2½ acres of land. When he dies, the fields will be divided among his four sons. But there won't be enough land for all of them to farm. Even now, only Uncle Khaled works in the fields with Ezzat's grandfather. Ezzat's father is a camel driver, and Uncle Abd el Aziz works in a local factory. Uncle Alaa is still looking for a job.

Ezzat's grandfather grows clover, wheat, beans, and corn. Ezzat's family eats the beans, but his grandfather sells the wheat and the corn. The clover is grown to feed the animals.

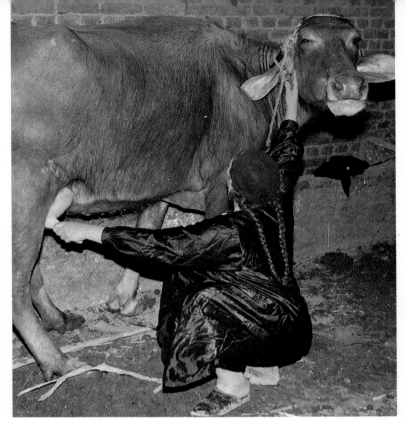

Including Ezzat's pet goat, the family has four goats, two donkeys, two *gamoosa*, or water buffalo, one camel, and lots of ducks and pigeons. Ezzat's father uses the camel for his work, and the donkeys are used to carry things and people, including Ezzat and his cousins.

The goats are raised as food, and the *gamoosa* give the family milk. *Gamoosa* are nervous animals, and only Ezzat's grandmother is able to milk them. She milks them twice a day. The milk that the family doesn't drink is used to make cheese or is sold to the village dairy.

The *gamoosa* work on the farm, too. They pull the plow through Grandfather's fields. They also turn the *sakia*, which is a heavy water wheel. The *gamoosa* walks around in a circle, pulling a pole which turns the water wheel. The wheel scoops up water from Grandfather's well and pours it into small channels cut into the fields.

The well is filled with water from the Nile, brought in by a long canal. Canals and drains carry water to and from fields and villages all along the Nile. Many of the canals were built thousands of years ago.

Some villagers use electric pumps to water their crops, but most of the farmers use *sakias*. They also use another kind of pump, the Archimedes' screw, which was invented over 2,000 years ago. Ezzat's grandfather uses it to pump small quantities of water from the canal into his fields. He puts one end of the pump into the water and turns the handle. Water is forced up the curved grooves inside the screw and out of the top.

Farmers need all these different ways of getting water from the Nile. Without water, they couldn't farm the land. Until 1966, the river used to flood every year. Now, a huge dam controls the level of the water. This means that farmers can grow crops all year round.

The family keeps the ducks in a small pen on the roof of their house. Pigeons are kept on the roof, too. They live in tall dovecotes made of mud. The ducks and pigeons aren't kept as pets. They are raised to be eaten. Roast pigeon is a favorite Egyptian dish.

The flat roofs of the village houses come in handy for storing food, firewood, animal fodder, and fertilizer. Dates and other kinds of food are laid out to dry on large flat trays woven from palm leaves. Old stalks of corn are also piled up on the roofs. Corn stalks make good fuel for the kitchen ovens.

Some families build small granaries on their roofs. Like the dovecotes, the granaries are made of mud. Dried dates, grain, flour, corn, onions, and other kinds of food are stored in them. The granaries keep the food safe from hungry birds or animals. Ezzat's pet goat is always escaping up the stairs onto the roof to lie in the warm sun.

15

Many people in Om Khenan grow date palms. They eat the sweet, sticky dates and use the thick trunks of the palm trees to build houses, carts, and stables.

The local farmers pay Ezzat's father to take their goods from place to place. Sometimes Ezzat's father loads up his camel with huge bundles of palm leaves. He takes the palm leaves into the village.

The palm leaves are woven into mats and baskets or used to make string and rope. Groups of village girls strip the palm leaves from the stems. The girls work so quickly that you can hardly see their hands.

The green palm stems are useful, too. You can see them stacked up against the walls of houses all over the village. After their leaves have been stripped off, the ends of the stems are beaten until they split into shreds. These shreds are made into brooms for sweeping houses.

The palm stems are also chopped up into small sticks and made into light crates and baskets. Many families in the village make crates to sell. The older men carefully split the palm stems into thin sticks. Then their children put the sticks into the holes of a frame which the men have made. The crates are used all over Egypt to transport food and other goods. Ezzat's family has even turned some crates into hanging baskets for the pigeons that live on the roof.

Many different goods are made in Om Khenan. People sit in their doorways and chat with each other while they work. The Archimedes' screw that Ezzat's grandfather uses was made by a craftsman in Om Khenan.

You can tell where the copper workshops are by the noise that comes from inside. The big sheets of copper are heated and then beaten into shape with a hammer. Some of the craftsmen collect old copper pots which have been thrown away by rich people in Cairo. Then they repair or remake them. Copper is too expensive to be wasted. The craftsmen have machines to polish the metal until it is shiny and bright.

A young bride is always given a collection of copper pans at her wedding. Ezzat's mother keeps her collection safe under her bed. Copper pans are very sturdy but they are also hard to clean.

Ezzat's mother now uses aluminum pans for cooking. But she uses a big copper bowl for washing clothes. Although Ezzat's house has running water, the women often do the laundry beside one of the small canals which run past Om Khenan. They like to sit with their friends while they work.

Ezzat's grandmother usually stays at home. She sits in the shady courtyard where the oven is. A stairway leads from the courtyard up to the roof. Sometimes she goes up to the roof to get food or fuel for the oven.

Today, Ezzat's grandmother is making the week's supply of bread. She takes grains of corn out of the basket beside her and puts them in the oven to roast. Then she grinds the roasted grains into flour. Ezzat's mother mixes the flour with water to make a sticky dough and spreads it out on a wooden board. When the dough has been baked for about two minutes, it turns into a flat loaf of bread. The family eats bread with almost every meal.

Ezzat's grandmother buys most of the family's food from street traders. They come right to her door with their goods loaded onto donkeys or wooden wheelbarrows. His grandmother, mother, and aunt share the cooking. Sometimes his sister helps them.

Ezzat's father and uncles eat their lunch at work. They usually have bread and cheese with tomatoes or onions. The main family meal is in the early evening after sunset. The women often prepare it in the morning. They cook meat and vegetables and serve them with rice, bread, or *foul*. *Foul* is made from beans and can be cooked many ways. One way is to crush the beans, add oil and lemon juice, and mix them into a paste.

21

If Ezzat's grandmother wants to buy something special, she sends Ezzat to the weekly market in Om Khenan. Every Thursday, the traders set up their stalls early in the morning. They sell many different kinds of foods, herbs, spices, and perfumes. Some of the stalls sell clay storage jars for water and grain. Others sell farming tools. There are beautiful carpets and pieces of cloth for sale. One trader sells bridles and saddles decorated with bells and tassels for use on camels, donkeys, and horses.

Ezzat likes to stop at the stall that sells children's toys. He can't spend much time there, though, because school starts at 7 A.M. Ezzat is in a class of 49 children. They go to the morning session. In the afternoon, another class uses the same room.

After school, Ezzat must finish his homework. Then he can play soccer with his friends or watch television. Ezzat loves soccer and is on the school team.

Ezzat looks forward to school vacations. Then he can play soccer every day. His grandfather rarely asks him to help on the farm. Farther north in Egypt, children usually have to work during school vacations. They help their parents pick cotton. Cotton plants are short, so children can easily reach the balls of cotton. Cotton is Egypt's most important crop.

23

Ezzat and his family are Muslims. Like most people in Egypt, they follow the religion of Islam and worship at a mosque. Muslims believe in one God called Allah. There are also Christian families in Om Khenan.

Friday is a Muslim holiday. It's Ezzat's day off school. Every Friday at noon, he goes to the mosque to pray. His mother, grandmother, and aunt do not go with him. Muslim women usually pray at home.

Five times a day, a man called a *muezzin* calls the villagers to come to the mosque to pray. People who are working in the fields stop and pray where they are. When Muslims pray, they always kneel and turn toward Mecca, a city in Saudi Arabia. Mecca is the holiest city in the religion of Islam. Muslims from all over the world go there.

Some of the people in Ezzat's village have been to Mecca. They have painted pictures of their journey on the walls of their houses. Their pictures show the camels, donkeys, ships, or airplanes which took them to Mecca. Some people have painted pictures of the mosques in Mecca or have written verses from the Koran, the holy book of Islam.

Ezzat has never been to Mecca, but he hopes to go there some day. He has been to Cairo, though. His father took him to the camel market there. Ezzat had never seen so many camels in one place before!

Every week, hundreds of camels are sold at the market. Some are sold to camel drivers like Ezzat's father. Others are sold for their meat.

The camels come from the Sudan, a country south of Egypt. They have to walk a long way across the desert to get to Cairo.

Ezzat likes the noise and bustle of Cairo, but he doesn't want to live there. He prefers his small village.

The two things Ezzat enjoys most right now are playing cards with his friend Mohamed and playing soccer. He and Mohamed play soccer almost every evening. Sometimes Mohamed's little sister joins them.

By 6 P.M., the sun has set and Ezzat is back home having supper. Afterwards, he usually watches television until it's time for bed. Then he dreams of soccer.

Ancient Egypt

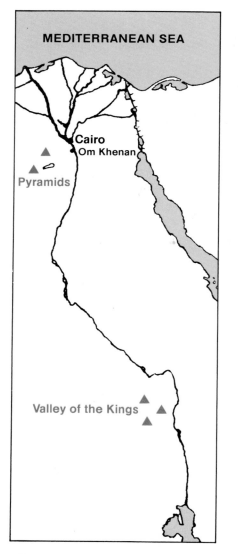

MEDITERRANEAN SEA

Cairo
Om Khenan

Pyramids

Valley of the Kings

Egypt's history dates back more than 5,000 years. Long before other parts of the world were civilized, life in ancient Egypt included art, literature, science, and math.

Ancient Egyptians believed in life after death, and it was very important to them that when they died their bodies were kept safe. Some of the kings built pyramids to use as tombs. Over 80 of these pyramids still stand, some not far from Ezzat's village.

One of the most famous tombs of ancient Egypt belonged to the ruler Tutankhamun, or King Tut. Tut's tomb was not housed in a pyramid but was cut into the rock in the Valley of the Kings, about 400 miles (250 kilometers) south of Cairo. It was discovered less than 70 years ago. Found in it were jewelry, furniture, dishes, and other beautiful objects—and the body of King Tut, preserved as a mummy for over 3,200 years!

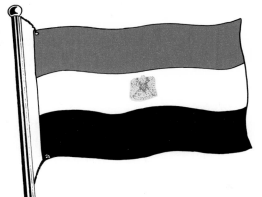

Facts about Egypt

Capital: Cairo

Language: Arabic

Form of Money: the Egyptian pound

Area: 386,662 square miles
(1,001,449 square kilometers)
The United States, including
Alaska and Hawaii, is about ten
times the size of Egypt.

Population: about 46 million people
There are about five times more
people in the United States than
there are in Egypt.

NORTH
AMERICA

SOUTH
AMERICA

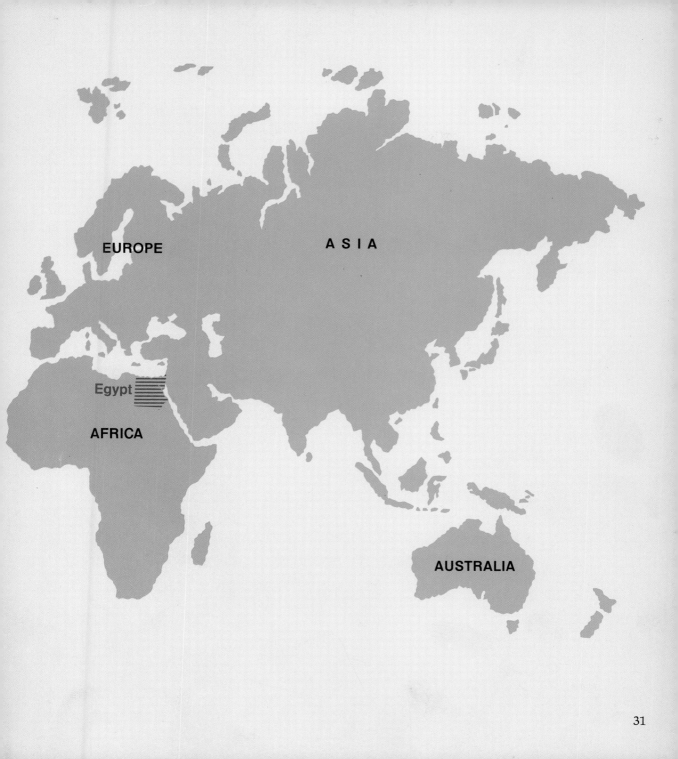

EUROPE

ASIA

Egypt

AFRICA

AUSTRALIA

FAMILIES AROUND THE WORLD

Some children in foreign countries live like you do. Others live very differently. In these books, you can meet children from all over the world. You'll learn about their games and schools, their families and friends, and what it's like to grow up in a faraway land.

A FAMILY IN CHINA

A FAMILY IN EGYPT

A FAMILY IN FRANCE

A FAMILY IN INDIA

A FAMILY IN JAMAICA

A FAMILY IN NIGERIA

A FAMILY IN PAKISTAN

A FAMILY IN SRI LANKA

A FAMILY IN WEST GERMANY

AN ABORIGINAL FAMILY

AN ARAB FAMILY

AN ESKIMO FAMILY

Lerner Publications Company
241 First Avenue North
Minneapolis, Minnesota 55401